A LIFEGUIDE® BIBLE STUDY

JEREMIAH
Demanding Love

*12 Studies
for individuals or groups*

Stephen D. Eyre

With Notes for Leaders

InterVarsity Press
Downers Grove, Illinois

InterVarsity Press® is the book-publishing division of InterVarsity Christian Fellowship®, a student movement active on campus at hundreds of universities, colleges and schools of nursing in the United States of America, and a member movement of the International Fellowship of Evangelical Students. For information about local and regional activities, write Public Relations Dept., InterVarsity Christian Fellowship, 6400 Schroeder Rd., P.O. Box 7895, Madison, WI 53707-7895.

Cover photograph: Dennis Flaherty

ISBN 0-8308-1030-7

Printed in the United States of America ♾

21	20	19	18	17	16	15	14	13	12	11	10	9	8	7	6	5	4	3	2	1
13	12	11	10	09	08	07	06	05	04	03	02	01	00	99	98	97	96			

Contents

Getting the Most from LifeGuide® Bible Studies   5

Introducing Jeremiah   8

1	Jeremiah 1	The Call of Jeremiah	11
2	Jeremiah 7:1-20	The Temple of Doom	14
3	Jeremiah 13:1-17	The Linen Belt	17
4	Jeremiah 18:1-17	The Potter's House	20
5	Jeremiah 23:1-24	The Righteous Branch	23
6	Jeremiah 24	The Basket of Figs	26
7	Jeremiah 25:15-38	The Cup of God's Wrath	29
8	Jeremiah 27	The Yoke of Babylon	32
9	Jeremiah 28	The Yoke of False Prophets	35
10	Jeremiah 32:1-25	The Field of Hope	38
11	Jeremiah 33	The Sure & Certain Promise	41
12	Jeremiah 38	The Not So Final End	44

Leader's Notes   47

Getting the Most
from LifeGuide® Bible Studies

Many of us long to fill our minds and our lives with Scripture. We desire to be transformed by its message. LifeGuide® Bible Studies are designed to be an exciting and challenging way to do just that. They help us to be guided by God's Word in every area of life.

How They Work

LifeGuides have a number of distinctive features. Perhaps the most important is that they are *inductive* rather than *deductive*. In other words, they lead us to *discover* what the Bible says rather than simply *telling* us what it says.

They are also thought-provoking. They help us to think about the meaning of the passage so that we can truly understand what the author is saying. The questions require more than one-word answers.

The studies are personal. Questions expose us to the promises, assurances, exhortations and challenges of God's Word. They are designed to allow the Scriptures to renew our minds so that we can be transformed by the Spirit of God. This is the ultimate goal of all Bible study.

The studies are versatile. They are designed for student, neighborhood and church groups. They are also effective for individual study.

How They're Put Together

LifeGuides also have a distinctive format. Each study need take no more than forty-five minutes in a group setting or thirty minutes in personal study—unless you choose to take more time.

The studies can be used within a quarter system in a church and fit well in a semester or trimester system on a college campus. If a guide has more than thirteen studies, it is divided into two or occasionally three parts of approximately twelve studies each.

LifeGuides use a workbook format. Space is provided for writing answers to each question. This is ideal for personal study and allows group members to prepare in advance for the discussion. The studies also contain leader's notes. They show how to lead a group discussion, provide additional background information on certain questions, give helpful tips on group dynamics and suggest ways to deal with problems which may arise during the discussion. With such helps, someone with little or no experience can lead an effective study.

Suggestions for Individual Study

1. As you begin each study, pray that God will help you to understand and apply the passage to your life.

2. Read and reread the assigned Bible passage to familiarize yourself with what the author is saying. In the case of book studies, you may want to read through the entire book prior to the first study. This will give you a helpful overview of its contents.

3. A good modern translation of the Bible, rather than the King James Version or a paraphrase, will give you the most help. The New International Version, the New American Standard Bible and the Revised Standard Version are all recommended. However, the questions in this guide are based on the New International Version.

4. Write your answers in the space provided in the study guide. This will help you to express your understanding of the passage clearly.

5. It might be good to have a Bible dictionary handy. Use it to look up any unfamiliar words, names or places.

Suggestions for Group Study

1. Come to the study prepared. Follow the suggestions for individual study mentioned above. You will find that careful preparation will greatly enrich your time spent in group discussion.

2. Be willing to participate in the discussion. The leader of your group will not be lecturing. Instead, he or she will be encouraging the members of the group to discuss what they have learned from the passage. The leader will be asking the questions that are found in this guide. Plan to share what God has taught you in your individual study.

3. Stick to the passage being studied. Your answers should be based on the verses which are the focus of the discussion and not on outside authorities such as commentaries or speakers. This guide deliberately avoids jumping

from book to book or passage to passage. Each study focuses on only one passage. Book studies are generally designed to lead you through the book in the order in which it was written. This will help you follow the author's argument.

4. Be sensitive to the other members of the group. Listen attentively when they share what they have learned. You may be surprised by their insights! Link what you say to the comments of others so the group stays on the topic. Also, be affirming whenever you can. This will encourage some of the more hesitant members of the group to participate.

5. Be careful not to dominate the discussion. We are sometimes so eager to share what we have learned that we leave too little opportunity for others to respond. By all means participate! But allow others to also.

6. Expect God to teach you through the passage being discussed and through the other members of the group. Pray that you will have an enjoyable and profitable time together.

7. If you are the discussion leader, you will find additional suggestions and helpful ideas for each study in the leader's notes. These are found at the back of the guide.

Introducing Jeremiah

As a teenager, I was delighted when my pastor started a series of sermons on prophecy. I hadn't been a Christian very long, and I had the impression that the Bible was a mysterious book that spoke about the future. I suppose at that time you could say that I put the Bible, Edgar Casey and the works of Nostradamus in the same category.

My pastor brought some cold water to my youthful fancy. I learned that the future the prophets spoke about wasn't primarily some distant utopia that had to be deciphered by hocus pocus and hidden wisdom. Instead, I learned that the prophets of the Old Testament were only partly concerned with the future. Their primary focus was on calling God's people back to faithful obedience and worship. When the prophets spoke of the future, they did so to let Israel know that they could expect defeat at the hands of their enemies if they didn't repent.

This was not at all what I expected. As my pastor developed the series, the prophets seemed to me to be strange characters wandering around thundering the message of an angry God to people who refused to obey him. After that series, I wasn't so eager to talk about prophecy anymore. I wasn't sure I liked the prophets or their message.

Eventually I got back to the prophets in my personal study. I was convinced that if the prophets were in the Scriptures, then I needed to study them. What I discovered at that time was that, yes, many of the prophets did strange things and proclaimed of lots of wrath. What was off in my understanding, however, was the impression I got of God.

The thundering message of judgment came not because God is a short-tempered despot shouting angry curses at people who break his rules, but because he is so intensely caring for those he gave himself to. In and through the message of the prophets as they proclaimed the coming judgment is a message of love. I like the way the prophet Jeremiah says it: "I have loved you with an everlasting love; I have drawn you with loving-kindness" (31:3).

In this guide we will find the prophet Jeremiah behaving strangely—proclaiming wrath and impending destruction. Jeremiah lived and wrote in a dark time. For over 250 years God had been sending prophets to warn his people to change their ways. And for over 250 years the prophets were ignored, persecuted or killed. As Jeremiah began his ministry somewhere around 620 B.C. God had already sent the northern half of the kingdom into exile a hundred years previous. Jeremiah was the last messenger for the southern kingdom, their very last chance to turn things around. God and Jeremiah knew that it wouldn't work, but they rebuked and proclaimed anyway.

Studying the ministry of the prophet Jeremiah, you will get a glimpse of what it is like to have a personal relationship with God. God called Jeremiah to a painful ministry. But with that great burden he gave Jeremiah a great gift, the gift of himself. When you study Jeremiah you get a glimpse of what it can be like for God and a human to be together. You will see a message of love that grows from a relationship of love—a hard love, a demanding love, but love nevertheless. What you will also discover, if you pay attention, is how you can grow in your own personal relationship to God. You will be stronger and more deeply open to the love of God than you were before.

The Shape of the Study
The book of Jeremiah is challenging. It is the second longest of all the prophetic works, with fifty-two chapters. There are three major sections:

□ Jeremiah 1—20   The Impending Judgment
□ Jeremiah 21—45   Living in the Midst of God's Judgment
□ Jeremiah 46—52   Oracles of International Judgment

We will study the first two sections. The last section is a collection of sermons on various topics. We can get at the heart of Jeremiah's message by focusing on the first two sections.

How shall we select among the forty-five chapters of the first two sections? One of the ways that Jeremiah sought to get his message across was through the use of symbols. At one time he stands at the door of the temple and uses it as a backdrop. At another time he uses a linen belt, another time a potter's house, then a clay jar, later a basket of figs and then a yoke. We will look at these symbols and the messages that accompany them.

As we ponder the symbols of Jeremiah, we will touch on the following themes of his ministry:

☐ the defamation of the temple and the false practice of religion

☐ the breaking of the covenant bond with God

☐ the right of God to judge Judah for their sin

☐ Judah's spiritual adultery with the gods

☐ the failure of Judah's spiritual leaders

☐ God's promised blessing for the captives

☐ God's judgment of all the nations

☐ Jeremiah's experience of opposition from the false prophets

☐ God's promise to restore people to the land after the period of judgment

Through all the symbols and themes and the proclamations of judgment there is a commitment of love. Through Jeremiah, God says:

I will make an everlasting covenant with them: I will never stop doing good to them, and I will inspire them to fear me, so that they will never turn away from me. I will rejoice in doing them good and will assuredly plant them in this land with all my heart and soul.

This is what the LORD says: As I have brought all this great calamity on this people, so I will give them all the prosperity I have promised them. (32:40-42)

When you stop to think about it, the prophets do speak of the future. God promised Israel a future on the other side of judgment and sin. It will be a time of peace, love and prosperity. A time of joy beyond which we can hardly imagine. The good news is that he invites those who have joined his people through faith in his son, Jesus Christ, to that future as well.

1
The Call of Jeremiah: Prophet to the Nations

Jeremiah 1

Maybe it's because I was in college in the sixties, but I've always wanted to do something significant with my life, to change the world. For this reason, coming into a relationship with God through Jesus Christ after my freshman year was exciting. What could be more meaningful than giving my life to God?

I've been following him for a couple of decades now. I have found it meaningful and fulfilling. But I discovered something else. Doing something significant wasn't quite what I thought it would be. Somehow I thought that making a difference would feel good and elicit loads of affirmation and appreciation from others. Well, sometimes it does and sometimes it doesn't!

Jeremiah was called by God to a life of great meaning and significance. He also found lots of trouble. Why then did he do it? Read on and see.

1. Describe a time when you were given the opportunity to do something important. How did you feel?

2. Read Jeremiah 1. The first three verses set the historical context. Jeremiah's ministry lasted about forty years, through one good king and then two wicked ones. From verses 1-3 alone, what do you think his ministry might have been like?

---

3. Verse 1 begins, "The words of Jeremiah." Verse 2 begins, "The word of the LORD." What insight does this give you into the book you are beginning to study?

---

4. Describe Jeremiah's call in your own words (vv. 4-10).

---

5. How does the word of the Lord shape Jeremiah's identity (vv. 6-9)?

---

6. God's Word shapes the identity of all who hear it. How has it shaped you?

---

7. God addressed Jeremiah's fears of being too immature and inadequate. Are there ways that God has addressed your fears?

8. Jeremiah gets practice learning to see and hear God's word. What two pictures is he given, and what challenges does each present to the young prophet?

---

9. According to the second vision, Jeremiah is going to deliver a message of destruction. What is going to happen, and why will it take place?

---

10. Jeremiah's message will not be well received. What is the meaning of God's warning (vv. 17-19)?

---

11. How might God's promise of protection and expectation of obedience be helpful for the challenges you face?

---

12. As Christians, we are called to witness to Jesus Christ. In what way is that also a call to a prophetic ministry of judgment and grace?

2
The Temple of Doom: Empty Religion

Jeremiah 7:1-20

I am an ordained minster. I love the church. But there are days when I have my doubts about "organized" religion. I'm not exactly proud of the Crusades, the treatment of the Jews in the Middle Ages or the more recent fundraising scandals of the television evangelists. There are times when it seems that politics, power and social concerns are the primary moving and shaping forces of our churches.

I am reminded on occasion that all that is done in the name of the Lord is not from the Lord. Jeremiah called the people of Judah to examine their motives for their religious pursuits. One day his challenge took place in front of the newly renovated temple. What a shock it must have been for those who heard.

We would all do well to stop and evaluate our motives for our spiritual pursuits. Jeremiah calls us to ponder: "Why do I serve God? Why am I going to church?"

---

1. What would you do if someone stood at the door of your newly renovated church and told you and everyone who entered that you were hypocrites under the judgment of God?

---

2. Read Jeremiah 7:1-11. Jeremiah stands at the door of the temple and confronts those who enter. What is his message?

___

3. In verse 4 Jeremiah repeats the phrase "The temple of the LORD" three times. What do you think he is getting at?

___

4. Jeremiah says that the words "The temple of the LORD" are deceptive. What is deceptive about them?

___

5. Under the reign of Josiah, Judah's last good king, the temple had been renovated and the law, which had been lost, was rediscovered. How "law abiding" do the people seem to be (vv. 5-11)?

___

6. In verse 11 God declares that he is watching. If God were to tell you that he was especially watching your church, what do you think he would see and say?

___

7. Read Jeremiah 7:12-20. How does the experience of Shiloh illustrate Jeremiah's message?

8. God, not the temple, should have been the object of their faith. How is it possible that focus could shift from a person, God, to an object, like the temple?

9. Jeremiah confronted the social injustice that made their worship unacceptable. In verses 16-20 he confronts their idolatry. How widespread was it?

10. God was angry with their idolatry and promised to judge it. Why do you think he was so upset with their false worship?

What does this say about his relationship to his people?

11. God charges that the whole family was involved in idolatrous worship. In light of our study of Jeremiah's message, what can we do to see that our family worships in a way that is pleasing to God?

12. What can we do to see that our own personal worship is pleasing to God?

3
The Linen Belt: Spoiled Bond

Jeremiah 13:1-17

Firm commitments are an important part of our lives. The bank you borrow money from wants to know your credit record and your assets to see if you can keep your commitment to repay your loan. And be careful about your business partners. Can they keep a commitment? You sign a binding contract with someone who has a history of breaking them at your peril. Think long and hard about the commitment marriage involves. Marry someone who has series of former partners and the chances are good that you will end up with a broken heart.

God especially doesn't like those who make commitments of convenience. He has high standards for us and for himself. When he makes a commitment, he stakes his life on it. Jesus Christ is the evidence. He expects the same sort of fidelity in return. Just as there are painful consequences when a business contract is broken or when a marriage partner cheats, so there are painful consequences when we default on our commitments to God.

---

1. What were the consequences of someone failing to keep their commitment to you?

How did you feel?

2. Read Jeremiah 13:1-17. Describe the task that God gave to Jeremiah in verses 1-11.

3. What is the point of this object lesson?

4. What is God's complaint (vv. 9-11)?

5. One purpose of a belt is to tie things together. What things might come apart in your life if you were no longer bound to the Lord?

6. A linen belt was more than functional; it was an ornament of dignity and pride. How might Israel and Judah have been a source of pride to God?

7. God wants to take pride in a relationship with his people. How can this insight enrich your relationship with him?

8. In contrast to the previous study, Jeremiah's message in verses 12-17 is directed at the leaders. In what ways is pride and arrogance a problem?

9. What do the images of drunkenness and darkness (vv. 13, 16) communicate about the coming judgment?

10. What could be the remedy for the coming judgment (vv. 15-17)?

11. Giving glory to God puts the focus back on him and puts us in our proper place. Consider giving glory to God for yourself, your family, your work and your whole course of life. How does this alter the way that you think about them?

12. Jeremiah calls the leaders to turn from arrogance by listening to the Lord (v. 15). How can God's Word be a remedy for our inclination to foolish pride?

13. How can God's Word strengthen our bonds and commitments?

4
The Potter's House: God's Shaping Hand

Jeremiah 18:1-17

One of my sons just got braces. He is not happy about it. For the next three years his mouth is going to be full of metal and rubber bands that push and pull his teeth and jaw back into shape. Three years seems like a long time, but moving flesh and bone is difficult. Braces are inconvenient and painful, but they will improve my son's mouth and health for the rest of his life.

God is interested in shaping us, not just our teeth, but our whole being. It's a big task. Shaping souls is difficult, takes time and requires divine power and skills. Unlike gums, teeth and bone, souls don't always yield to the shaping pressures of the divine hand. If they do, it takes a lifetime of God's pressures to conform to the end goal, the image of Christ.

Jeremiah didn't know about braces, nor did he know the name of Jesus Christ, but he did know that God is in the business of shaping our lives.

---

1. Recall one or two major events that have been a significant shaping influence in your life. How did they affect you for good or for ill?

---

2. Read Jeremiah 18:1-17. What did Jeremiah see and hear at the potter's house (vv. 1-10)?

3. God draws a comparison between himself and the potter, who can do what he likes. How would you think God might respond to someone who objects that this isn't fair?

4. God makes it clear that his pronouncements and promises are conditional. How do you think God might respond to someone who objects that this makes him untrustworthy?

5. Jeremiah draws an analogy between human nations and clay in the potter's hand. How does the difference between humans and clay make this an analogy of hope?

6. Being reshaped by the divine potter isn't always a pleasant experience. Describe one or two times when you have been aware of God's shaping hand in your life.

7. In order to be reshaped by the potter, the clay has to be soft. How well is Judah going to do under God's hand (vv. 11-15)?

8. Israel had a reputation of being protected and cared for by its powerful God. How is Israel's reputation going to change?

9. In verse 12 Judah responds to God's warning with the reply "It's no use." What do you think that means?

10. A primary cause of Judah's coming judgment was a determined forgetfulness (v. 15). How might forgetfulness be an expression of disobedience and unfaithfulness?

11. Judah was a nation with a hard heart that expressed itself in disobedience and idolatry. How would you describe the behavior of a person with a hard heart?

a person with a soft heart?

12. God is the one who shapes us. How has God spoken to you in this passage about the way he is shaping you?

5
The Righteous Branch: A Divine Coup

Jeremiah 23:1-24

During World War II, the Japanese experimented with effective ways to run their prison camps. At one camp they removed the five percent of the prison population that had any experience in leadership or who could articulate a defined set of religious beliefs and moral behavior. The results were amazing. There were less attempted escapes and more docile prisoners at that camp than at any of their others.

We need leaders and we need beliefs. But what happens when the leaders become corrupt or intentionally lead in an immoral way? Judah faced just such a crisis. The whole nation was headed for a cliff, and the leaders weren't doing anything about it. In fact, they were leading the way to the edge. How will God respond? Jeremiah has some bad news for the leaders and some good news for the people.

1. Recall someone who has been an influential leader in your life. What did they do and how did it affect you?

2. Read Jeremiah 23:1-24. Verses 1-8 describe what could be called a second exodus. How will it be different from the first one?

3. God promises a new ruler from the line of David (vv. 5-8). How will his reign be different from the current leaders' (vv. 9-22)?

4. God himself promises to provide new leadership as Israel's shepherd king. How is that promise fulfilled in Jesus Christ?

5. The shepherd king is called "The LORD Our Righteousness" (v. 6). How is that promise also fulfilled in Jesus Christ?

6. What one or two ways have you experienced the benefits of the Lord as your shepherd and your righteousness?

7. What charges are brought against the religious leaders (vv. 9-24)?

8. What are the results of their leadership?

9. How will the punishment fit the crime for Israel's leaders (vv. 1-4)?

10. If God were to bring charges against the spiritual leaders of today's church, what do think they might be?

What effects might such leadership be having on the life of the church and individual Christians?

11. The prophet and priest look to the Baals and their own conjured-up dreams, rather than to the Lord. What false gods might wayward spiritual leaders be looking to today?

12. God charges the religious leaders with failing to stand in his council (vv. 18, 22). We may not be prophets or priests, but we can learn from their example. How do you receive the counsel of the Lord?

What benefits might that bring in your life and in those around you?

6
The Basket of Figs: Living with God's Judgment

Jeremiah 24

After the evening service, a visiting preacher was invited to spend the night at the home of one of the wealthy members of the church. The host was proud of his new house and showed it off with obvious pride. He attributed his good fortune to the Lord, saying that God had blessed his business in the previous year with a fourfold increase in profits.

The guest was not impressed. With a dismissive gesture he asked his host, "How do you know that your prosperity is not a trick of the devil to cause you to become proud, materialistic and greedy?"

Although the challenge of the preacher seems harsh, it's a good question. What appears to be good fortune at the present may not be so in the end. In Jeremiah's message to the exiles and those who stayed in the land after the first deportation in A.D. 596, he turns the concept of good fortune on its head and provides a different perspective.

---

1. When have you changed your mind about what you initially thought was a great opportunity or positive development?

---

2. Read Jeremiah 24. Jeremiah is shown a vision of figs. What is the historical context in which Jeremiah sees this vision (v. 1)?

How does this vision of the figs display the continuing presence and power of God in the midst of a time of military defeat for Judah?

---

3. How does the vision of the figs change the way you might think about those who were taken in captivity to Babylon and those who got to stay in Jerusalem (vv. 5-10)?

---

4. God says that he is going to regard the exiles as "good" (v. 5). What might that mean?

---

5. What commitments does God make to the exiles?

---

6. How is God's watching, mentioned in verse 6, different from the references to his watching that we studied in 1:12 and 7:11?

7. Christians are to consider themselves blessed by God in the midst of difficult circumstances. What can we learn from the experience of the exiles that can help us experience God's blessing in difficult times?

8. What are some of the benefits that you have received from trying times?

9. How might those who escaped captivity feel about themselves, the exiles and God (vv. 8-10)?

10. Look at the description in verses 9-10 of what will happen to those who stay. Why do you think God is harsh with them?

11. The experience of good fortune now doesn't always reflect ultimate reality. What wisdom can we draw from this act of God's judgment?

12. God's ultimate act of judgment that turns everything upside down is the resurrection. How does that affect the way Christians are to consider the terrible experience of death and the struggles of this life?

7
The Cup of God's Wrath: International Judgment

Jeremiah 25:15-38

I know lots of people who want to believe in "the God of the New Testament." He is described by those people as a God of love. In contrast, many do not want to believe in the Old Testament God. He is thought of as a God of wrath who punishes people for disobedience and sends wars on those who don't obey him.

In this chapter we face the issue of the God of wrath head-on. Through Jeremiah, God proclaims a war caused by the "cup of God's wrath" that will bring death and destruction among the nations. What you are about to read is painful and unsettling.

What most people who want to dismiss the Old Testament God don't know, however, is that the cup of wrath sent by God in the Old Testament continues right over into the New Testament. In the garden of Gethsemane Jesus takes the cup and drinks it for us (Mt 26:39).

As painful as this passage is, we need it to understand the work of God in his world.

---

1. How do you respond when you hear someone say that God is a God of love but not a God of wrath?

2. Read Jeremiah 25:15-38. The central image of this portion of Jeremiah is the cup of God's wrath. Who is the cup for?

_____

3. There is an extensive list of nations in verses 18-26. What is God's point in mentioning them one by one?

_____

4. The nations don't have a choice about this coming war. What is the reason for God's wide-ranging judgment (vv. 27-29)?

_____

5. What does it say about God that he is willing to judge his own people as well as the rest of the nations?

_____

6. Verses 30-33 emphasize the sounds of war. What will be heard, and what will the sounds mean?

_____

7. War is a terrible thing. How is it merely a symptom of the real problem of the human race?

8. What justification can there be for God to cause such terrible experiences?

9. In most wars, one or even both sides claim that God is on their side. How might you respond to such a claim in light of Jeremiah's prophecy?

10. Jeremiah uses the images of a shepherd and a lion to describe the leaders and God. How does that help the leaders understand their situation (vv. 34-38)?

11. Consider wars in the twentieth century—World War I, World War II, Vietnam, the Gulf War or other wars that come to mind. How do you think leaders of the nations involved viewed their participation in them?

12. Those who were to experience the impending war were in for a terrible experience. What consolation is there as we read these words of Jeremiah?

8
The Yoke of Babylon: How to Prosper Anyway

Jeremiah 27

Hiking along a narrow ledge on a path in the Alps, a tourist slipped and fell. Just before sliding off a cliff and down into the deep ravine below, he grabbed a tree root and hung on. About five minutes later, across the ravine, he heard a voice calling out, "Let go of the tree and swing to the left."

That didn't sound like a good idea, so he continued to cling to the tree. His hands were beginning to ache and his grip was slipping. The voice called out again: "Let go of the tree and swing to the left. From where I am standing I can see a ledge about twenty feet below you and just off at an angle. If you drop down you can get back to the path and walk down."

The hiker had to make a decision. Did he trust the voice or not? After all, how did he know that the voice was telling the truth? From where he hung it looked like a straight drop of hundreds of feet down to certain death. On the other hand, he couldn't hang on much longer.

Judah was in a difficult situation, hanging from a cliff, as it were, and getting strange advice from Jeremiah. Like the voice from across the ravine his message went against common sense and everything they understood about being the special people of God. Would they believe him and let go?

---

1. How do you evaluate and respond to advice from others?

2. Read Jeremiah 27:1-11. Jeremiah continues to function as a prophet to the nations. What is his message, and who is he speaking to?

3. Jeremiah also continues his use of images and object lessons. What was the purpose of giving the leaders in the Jerusalem counsel an object lesson with the yoke and a message about the coming power of Babylon?

4. How do you think the counsel of kings and envoys would have responded when Jeremiah walked in with a yoke on his neck?

5. Describe the difficult situation that Jeremiah's message puts the leaders in.

6. Read Jeremiah 27:12-22. Zedekiah received the same message as the nations. Why would this be especially upsetting and confusing to the nation who considered themselves to be God's chosen people (vv. 12-15)?

7. What challenge does Jeremiah issue to the prophets (v. 18)?

8. According to Jeremiah, the remainder of the temple furnishings were going to be taken to Babylon. How would you feel if the pulpit, cross and other important items of worship were taken from your church?

---

9. How does God communicate that he is in charge of the whole experience of Judah's defeat (vv. 21-22)?

---

10. God is both the source of Judah's judgment and the means of their deliverance. How then could this knowledge provide wisdom and guidance for the leaders and the people?

---

11. When you are going through difficult times, what comfort and wisdom does the knowledge of God provide for you?

---

12. Jeremiah called the counsel members to risk going against common sense to receive God's deliverance. What risks has following God meant for you?

How can Jeremiah's courage be an example for you in the challenges you face?

9
The Yoke of False Prophets: Destroying False Hope

Jeremiah 28

How do God's people handle hostility? John the Baptist told his listeners they should go the second mile. Jesus told the disciples to turn the other cheek.

There is a tension here. We may be inclined to think that Christians should be doormats, giving way to the forces of hostile opposition. But that is not the point. Jesus confronted the religious leaders with their hypocrisy and called for the judgment of God on them. Matthew 23 records some of his hot rhetoric. Yet, while Jesus confronted, he didn't lead a jihad, a holy war, to destroy the opposition. He trusted God to bring judgment and justice in his way and his time.

Jeremiah's ministry was full of confrontation and hostility from the opposition. In this study it becomes physical and deadly. As we watch Jeremiah, we can learn how to trust God's guidance and power in threatening situations.

---

1. What would you do if someone confronted you in public and tried to humiliate and discredit you?

2. Read Jeremiah 28:1-9. The conflict begins when Hananiah confronts Jeremiah in the temple. How would you describe the interaction between Jeremiah and Hananiah?

3. How do you think Hananiah's message was received by the priests and people (vv. 1-4)?

4. How would you characterize Jeremiah's initial response to Hananiah (vv. 5-9)?

5. Summarize Jeremiah's rebuttal to Hananiah.

6. The people who hear Jeremiah and Hananiah must choose who they believe is actually speaking the word of the Lord. What test does Jeremiah give for discerning a true prophet?

7. According to Jeremiah, how is Hananiah's prophecy different from all the other prophets who preceded him?

8. How can we know that the words recorded in the Bible are really words from God and not merely human words of empty hopes and dreams?

---

9. Read Jeremiah 28:10-17. Shortly after Hananiah broke the yoke off Jeremiah's neck, the Lord gave Jeremiah a stern rebuttal for Hananiah. Why might he have waited for a period of time instead of speaking when Hananiah broke the yoke?

---

10. Jeremiah's rebuttal sets up a stark test of his ministry. Why do you think God's response was so harsh?

---

11. What do you think those who heard the encounter between Jeremiah and Hananiah might have learned?

---

12. What have you learned in this passage about being faithful to God's Word in your life?

---

13. What insight does this incident between Jeremiah and Hananiah provide in spotting false prophets or misleading messages given by false teachers?

10
The Field of Hope: The Promise of Renewed Land

Jeremiah 32:1-25

Sociologists have discovered a set of behaviors which they call "deferred gratification pattern." It describes the practice of putting off a purchase or action in hope that better dividends would come in the future. Most everyone who lives by deferred gratification expects to get a good return. But what if the benefits don't come in your lifetime?

In this chapter, Jeremiah makes a real-estate deal that on the surface looks foolish. It is the ultimate in deferred gratification. In the transaction he demonstrates the depth of his character, the strength of his maturity and the quality of his obedience to God.

---

1. How do you feel when you have to put off buying something that you really want immediately?

---

2. Read Jeremiah 32:1-25. Jerusalem is in a state of siege. How might Jeremiah's willingness to purchase a field have been a means of comfort to the threatened citizens?

3. Why is Jeremiah imprisoned in the courtyard, and why is Zedekiah shut up in Jerusalem?

---

4. Into this state of siege, Jeremiah is offered a real-estate deal from a relative. Why might it have been wise for Jeremiah to turn it down (vv. 6-12)?

---

5. Jeremiah's purchase of the field didn't fit with his message about sure and certain judgment. How do you think he felt about buying it?

---

6. Jeremiah records in detail the process of the legal transaction for the purchase of the land. What impact would this have on those who watched?

---

7. Why would Jeremiah make a transaction from which he would never personally benefit (vv. 14-15)?

---

8. What can we learn from Jeremiah's model about Christian service and character?

9. After the purchase Jeremiah offered a prayer (vv. 17-25). Under the circumstances, how might this have been a source of comfort for Jeremiah?

10. What themes are woven throughout the prayer?

11. How can prayer be a source of comfort for us in times of trouble and doubt?

12. Jeremiah's prayer shows a familiar knowledge of God's past actions. How can this study of Jeremiah be a resource for your prayers?

11
The Sure & Certain Promise

Jeremiah 33

W hen John the Baptist was in prison, he sent messengers to Jesus asking if he was the Messiah or not. The question probably came from confusion and despair. After all, hadn't John proclaimed the Coming One who would take away the sins of the world? Surely the Messiah's coming would bring freedom and fulfillment for everyone. How then could John be confined to prison? Something seemed wrong.

God had warned Jeremiah from the moment of his call that his ministry would be difficult. Even so, like John the Baptist, there must have been hard days of frustration and despair. He was ignored, rejected, despised and imprisoned. In the midst of that darkness, God comes to Jeremiah with a candle of light.

Sometimes God doesn't rescue us. Sometimes he does. Either way, he extends his love and grace.

---

1. When things look dark and depressing, what do you do to gain encouragement and hope?

---

2. Read Jeremiah 33:1-9. Jeremiah is imprisoned in Jerusalem with the Babylonian army at the gates. What does God do to offer him comfort?

3. The Hebrew meaning of the Lord's name used here is "Promise Keeper."
Why do you think God repeats his name four times in two verses?

4. Have there been times in your life when you felt confined, trapped or
limited?

How could or did the knowledge of God help?

5. God invites Jeremiah to call out for assurance and then immediately offers
his response (vv. 4-9). In what way would God's words be comforting?

6. God's answer gives both the bad news of Judah's defeat and the good
news of its restoration. How have you experienced both good and bad news
in your own relationship with God?

7. Look at verse 9. God is concerned about his reputation. How is that a
good thing for both God and his people?

8. Read Jeremiah 33:10-26. Describe the restoration promised for the city (vv. 10-11).

What is promised for the countryside (vv. 12-13)?

9. What is God going to do to fulfill his promises to Judah and Israel (vv. 15-18)?

How are those promises fulfilled in Jesus Christ?

10. The destruction of Israel and Judah could lead to the accusation that God was a covenant breaker. How does God answer this (vv. 20-26)?

11. What is the difference between a trustworthy God and a god who is fickle and impulsive?

12. God's people at the time of judgment had a restoration to look forward to. As Christians, what do we have to look forward to in times of trouble?

12
The Not So Final End: Sunk in the Mud

Jeremiah 38

With this passage we come to the end of our study of Jeremiah. Although the book goes on for another thirteen chapters, it is a fitting place to end because the chapter concludes with the final destruction and deportation of Judah in 586 B.C.

What a hard time it has been for Jeremiah! God warned him it would be difficult. Certainly it was, more than he ever imagined. In this passage we see Jeremiah thrown into the mud of a deep well and left for dead. Although he gets out of the well, he is not released from confinement and is imprisoned in Jerusalem until the very end.

The faith hall of fame is found in Hebrews 11. Jeremiah certainly qualifies. It is a record of godly men and women who trusted God when things looked dark or impossible. The author of Hebrews writes: "These were all commended for their faith, yet none of them received what had been promised. God had planned something better for us so that only together with us would they be made perfect" (11:39-40).

Jeremiah's ministry of faithfulness to God and God's people helped prepare the way for you and me. We can know God in ways that are deeper, richer and more powerful because Jeremiah had the courage to be faithful and the wisdom to record his words.

---

1. What sort of spiritual legacy would you like to leave for your friends and family?

2. Read Jeremiah 38:1-13. As Judah was being besieged by Babylon, what were Jeremiah's enemies concerned about?

3. If you were in leadership and heard Jeremiah's message, what would have to happen before you would be willing to surrender to your enemies?

4. Jeremiah ends up in the well, sunk down deep into the mud. How had God prepared Jeremiah for just such a situation?

5. In what ways can Christians end up in wells today?

How has God prepared us?

6. How did Jeremiah get out of the well (vv. 7-13)?

7. After giving permission for Jeremiah to be put in the well, the king gave

Ebed-Melech permission to take Jeremiah out of the well. Why do you think he changed his mind?

8. Read Jeremiah 38:14-28. Zedekiah the king calls Jeremiah to ask for his advice (vv. 14-23). What personal and political reasons does Jeremiah give for Zedekiah to surrender?

9. How might Jeremiah's experience in the cistern be a lesson for the king?

10. As Jerusalem faces its final destruction, the king and the prophet face each other. What do they have in common?

How are they different from each other?

11. Our study concludes with the final destruction of Jerusalem in 586. How would you evaluate the success of Jeremiah's ministry?

12. What lessons for your own life will you take from this study of Jeremiah?

Leader's Notes

Leading a Bible discussion can be an enjoyable and rewarding experience. But it can also be *scary*—especially if you've never done it before. If this is your feeling, you're in good company. When God asked Moses to lead the Israelites out of Egypt, he replied, "O Lord, please send someone else to do it!" (Ex 4:13).

When Solomon became king of Israel, he felt the task was beyond his abilities. "I am only a little child and do not know how to carry out my duties. . . . Who is able to govern this great people of yours?" (1 Kings 3:7, 9).

When God called Jeremiah to be a prophet, he replied, "Ah, Sovereign LORD, . . . I do not know how to speak; I am only a child" (Jer 1:6).

The list goes on. The apostles were "unschooled, ordinary men" (Acts 4:13). Timothy was young, frail and frightened. Paul's "thorn in the flesh" made him feel weak. But God's response to all of his servants—including you—is essentially the same: "My grace is sufficient for you" (2 Cor 12:9). Relax. God helped these people in spite of their weaknesses, and he can help you in spite of your feelings of inadequacy.

There is another reason why you should feel encouraged. Leading a Bible discussion is not difficult if you follow certain guidelines. You don't need to be an expert on the Bible or a trained teacher. The suggestions listed below should enable you to effectively and enjoyably fulfill your role as leader.

Preparing to Lead

1. Ask God to help you understand and apply the passage to your own life. Unless this happens, you will not be prepared to lead others. Pray too for the various members of the group. Ask God to give you an enjoyable and profitable time together studying his Word.

2. As you begin each study, read and reread the assigned Bible passage to familiarize yourself with what the author is saying. In the case of book studies, you may want to read through the entire book prior to the first study. This will give you a helpful overview of its contents.

3. This study guide is based on the New International Version of the Bible. It will help you and the group if you use this translation as the basis for your study and discussion. Encourage others to use the NIV also, but allow them the freedom to use whatever translation they prefer.

4. Carefully work through each question in the study. Spend time in meditation and reflection as you formulate your answers.

5. Write your answers in the space provided in the study guide. This will help you to express your understanding of the passage clearly.

6. It might help you to have a Bible dictionary handy. Use it to look up any unfamiliar words, names or places. (For additional help on how to study a passage, see chapter five of *Leading Bible Discussions,* IVP.)

7. Once you have finished your own study of the passage, familiarize yourself with the leader's notes for the study you are leading. These are designed to help you in several ways. First, they tell you the purpose the study guide author had in mind while writing the study. Take time to think through how the study questions work together to accomplish that purpose. Second, the notes provide you with additional background information or comments on some of the questions. This information can be useful if people have difficulty understanding or answering a question. Third, the leader's notes can alert you to potential problems you may encounter during the study.

8. If you wish to remind yourself of anything mentioned in the leader's notes, make a note to yourself below that question in the study.

Leading the Study

1. Begin the study on time. Unless you are leading an evangelistic Bible study, open with prayer, asking God to help you to understand and apply the passage.

2. Be sure that everyone in your group has a study guide. Encourage them to prepare beforehand for each discussion by working through the questions in the guide.

3. At the beginning of your first time together, explain that these studies are meant to be discussions not lectures. Encourage the members of the group to participate. However, do not put pressure on those who may be hesitant to speak during the first few sessions.

4. Read the introductory paragraph at the beginning of the discussion.

This will orient the group to the passage being studied.

5. Read the passage aloud if you are studying one chapter or less. You may choose to do this yourself, or someone else may read if he or she has been asked to do so prior to the study. Longer passages may occasionally be read in parts at different times during the study. Some studies may cover several chapters. In such cases reading aloud would probably take too much time, so the group members should simply read the assigned passages prior to the study.

6. As you begin to ask the questions in the guide, keep several things in mind. First, the questions are designed to be used just as they are written. If you wish, you may simply read them aloud to the group. Or you may prefer to express them in your own words. However, unnecessary rewording of the questions is not recommended.

Second, the questions are intended to guide the group toward understanding and applying the *main idea* of the passage. The author of the guide has stated his or her view of this central idea in the *purpose* of the study in the leader's notes. You should try to understand how the passage expresses this idea and how the study questions work together to lead the group in that direction.

There may be times when it is appropriate to deviate from the study guide. For example, a question may have already been answered. If so, move on to the next question. Or someone may raise an important question not covered in the guide. Take time to discuss it! The important thing is to use discretion. There may be many routes you can travel to reach the goal of the study. But the easiest route is usually the one the author has suggested.

7. Avoid answering your own questions. If necessary, repeat or rephrase them until they are clearly understood. An eager group quickly becomes passive and silent if they think the leader will do most of the talking.

8. Don't be afraid of silence. People may need time to think about the question before formulating their answers.

9. Don't be content with just one answer. Ask, "What do the rest of you think?" or "Anything else?" until several people have given answers to the question.

10. Acknowledge all contributions. Try to be affirming whenever possible. Never reject an answer. If it is clearly wrong, ask, "Which verse led you to that conclusion?" or again, "What do the rest of you think?"

11. Don't expect every answer to be addressed to you, even though this will probably happen at first. As group members become more at ease, they will begin to truly interact with each other. This is one sign of a healthy discussion.

12. Don't be afraid of controversy. It can be very stimulating. If you don't resolve an issue completely, don't be frustrated. Move on and keep it in mind for later. A subsequent study may solve the problem.

13. Stick to the passage under consideration. It should be the source for answering the questions. Discourage the group from unnecessary cross-referencing. Likewise, stick to the subject and avoid going off on tangents.

14. Periodically summarize what the *group* has said about the passage. This helps to draw together the various ideas mentioned and gives continuity to the study. But don't preach.

15. Conclude your time together with conversational prayer. Be sure to ask God's help to apply those things which you learned in the study.

16. End on time.

Many more suggestions and helps are found in *Leading Bible Discussions* (IVP). Reading and studying through that would be well worth your time.

Components of Small Groups

A healthy small group should do more than study the Bible. There are four components you should consider as you structure your time together.

Nurture. Being a part of a small group should be a nurturing and edifying experience. You should grow in your knowledge and love of God and each other. If we are to properly love God, we must know and keep his commandments (Jn 14:15). That is why Bible study should be a foundational part of your small group. But you can be nurtured by other things as well. You can memorize Scripture, read and discuss a book, or occasionally listen to a tape of a good speaker.

Community. Most people have a need for close friendships. Your small group can be an excellent place to cultivate such relationships. Allow time for informal interaction before and after the study. Have a time of sharing during the meeting. Do fun things together as a group, such as a potluck supper or a picnic. Have someone bring refreshments to the meeting. Be creative!

Worship. A portion of your time together can be spent in worship and prayer. Praise God together for who he is. Thank him for what he has done and is doing in your lives and in the world. Pray for each other's needs. Ask God to help you to apply what you have learned. Sing hymns together.

Mission. Many small groups decide to work together in some form of outreach. This can be a practical way of applying what you have learned. You can host a series of evangelistic discussions for your friends or neighbors. You can visit people at a home for the elderly. Help a widow with cleaning or repair jobs around her home. Such projects can have a transforming influence on your group.

For a detailed discussion of the nature and function of small groups, read *Small Group Leaders' Handbook* or *The Big Book on Small Groups* (both from IVP).

Study 1. Jeremiah 1. The Call of Jeremiah: Prophet to the Nations.

Purpose: To discover how God's call on our lives shapes and directs us.

Question 2. Josiah was the last good king of Israel. Josiah ruled thirty-one years and sought to bring about a spiritual renewal through the renovation of the temple and the proclamation of the Law (2 Chron 34—35). Johoiakim ruled eleven years (2 Chron 36:5-8), as did Zedekiah (2 Chron 36:11-21).

Being the son of a priest meant that Jeremiah was very possibly a priest himself. This is significant as several of Jeremiah's stunning messages of judgment are related to the temple. His thundering condemnations about the temple worship and the priests come not because he is a frustrated, alienated outsider but because those things which are most important to him are being destroyed by ungodly behavior. From beginning to end his ministry rings with integrity.

Question 5. Jeremiah would forever be marked by his calling to be a prophet. His life was to take on an adversarial role, confronting both the people and their leaders. Because of his calling, he would stand with God against the people. Not an easy task.

Question 6. We are shaped and defined by our values, our relationships and our sense of purpose. For Christians all these things arise from the Scriptures. For many church members our values, relationships and purpose are often not clearly conceived and articulated. This question will help to make explicit what is significant, but just below the surface.

Question 7. The objections of Jeremiah echo the words of Moses when he was called (Ex 3:11-13).

This question will call for some reflection and may even cause some discomfort. That's okay. Pause for a few moments to let people think. It requires an exercise of faith to discern ways that God has been active and supportive in the midst of the obstacles that we all face.

Question 8. Help your group understand that a call from God doesn't mean that everyone has to be a religious professional. One of the important teachings to come out of the Reformation was that every believer had a vocation, a calling from God. Teachers, lawyers, actors—whatever we do as a "career" should be understood by Christians as a calling from God as a means of our good and God's glory.

Question 9. The vision of the almond tree is a Hebrew play on words emphasizing that God is watching over his world. The word for "almond" sounds like the word for "watching." Jeremiah learns through this that what he sees from the Lord will be a key to what he is to hear.

An almond tree is the first to blossom in the spring. In the same way God will hasten to perform his words. Indications of God's work may seem scarce and the times long in coming, yet God's Word and judgment will certainly be fulfilled.

Question 10. The message of judgment comes because the law of God has been broken. In verse 16 the first and second commandment are singled out: "You shall have no other gods before me and you shall not make or worship idols" (see Ex 20:3-5). The root issue, however, is not merely that God's law has been broken, but that God himself has been rejected.

Question 11. God's commands bring strength and power with them. If God commands Jeremiah to be strong, then the ability to be strong will be present as well.

Study 2. Jeremiah 7:1-20. The Temple of Doom: Empty Religion.

Purpose: To see that God desires worship that comes from the heart.

Question 3. As Jeremiah delivers this stinging rebuke, keep in mind that he is probably a priest whose life and identity is tied to the temple. In fact it is possible that his father, Hilkiah, is the same one who is mentioned in 2 Kings 22—23 and was responsible for overseeing the renovation and restoration of the temple.

Question 4. The people of Judah were hiding behind their newly remodeled temple. While talking about their wonderful renewed building of the Lord, they were ignoring his commands and worshiping other gods. This self-deceit would not be tolerated by the Lord. Jeremiah was standing at the temple to confront them with their hypocrisy.

Question 5. Jeremiah mentions at least five of the Ten Commandments (Ex 20) as being broken. Both tables of the law—the responsibility toward God and toward fellow Israelites—were being ignored.

Question 6. The theme of watching was introduced with Jeremiah's first vision of the almond tree (1:11-12) and will come up again. God wants Judah to know that he sees them and knows what they are doing.

Question 8. Give people in the group time to think about this one. If you don't get a response after a moment's pause you might ask them to give their own perceptions first. The letters to the seven churches in Revelation 2 and

3 could provide some background how what Jesus thought of a group of churches in Asia Minor at the end of the first century.

Question 9. Although the ark and tabernacle were initally placed at Shiloh, eventually it ceased to be the place of Israel's worship. Likewise, the northern kingdom, in which Shiloh was located, had been taken into captivity by the Assyrians in 722 B.C. See Joshua 18:1; 22:12; Judges 21:19 and 1 Samuel 1:9, 24.

Question 12. This is an important question. It is not merely the rituals of worship that are important to God. He is committed to his people and wants their commitment in return. The root issue is one of God's love for his people. The people didn't love him and were in fact giving their love to someone else.

Question 13. When our boys were small, we listened to tapes of worship music on the way to church on Sunday morning. The music got us settled and focused after the weekly Sunday morning trauma of getting our children out the door so that we could get to church on time. It was on one of those drives that one of our boys made his first step in a personal commitment to Christ.

Praying with our children before they went to school and reminding them that God was the source of all that they were learning kept his presence before them on a daily basis. At bedtime we have used the Lord's Prayer as a basis for instruction and prayer. Together these small actions contributed to making Sunday morning worship of the Lord a focus and high point of our week.

Study 3. Jeremiah 13:1-17. The Linen Belt: Spoiled Bond.

Purpose: To think about the importance of keeping our commitments to God.

Question 2. We don't know where Perath, the place where the belt was buried, was located. Some commentators think it was as far away as Babylon. Others think it was located within the region of Judah.

Questions 3-6. In seeking to understand the message of the belt, keep in mind that a belt wasn't needed to hold up trousers. Trousers hadn't been invented yet!

Question 7. Many of us have a tendency to see God as a set of truths or an impersonal principle of goodness and truth. If we understand that God has feelings about us, that he can be pleased or displeased, it enriches our personal relationship with him.

Question 10. There is an important insight here into the nature of Jeremiah's ministry and God's purpose of pronouncing a coming judgment. God is not

sending Jeremiah to proclaim doom because he enjoys harassing Judah. He proclaims judgment with an eye toward repentance. If Judah knows what dangers await them, perhaps they will turn away from their unfaithfulness.
Question 11. Listening to and obeying God puts the focus back on him and puts us in our proper place. The key here is the image of glory. In contrast to darkness, glory brings light. In contrast to a staggering revelry of drunkenness, glory brings celebration, and in contrast to the arrogance of position, glory shifts the focus to God.

Study 4. The Potter's House: God's Shaping Hand. Jeremiah 18:1-17.
Purpose: To see that God offers us the opportunity to repent from sinful ways.
Question 3. The objection of fairness is addressed by the apostle Paul in Romans 9:14-25. The issue of fairness misses the point. God, as Creator, can do what he likes. However, to his glory and our benefit, he is both just and merciful. If we appeal to a sense of fairness and justice, then there is no hope for any of us. As the apostle Paul wrote, "All have sinned and fall short of the glory of God" (Rom 3:23), and "The wages of sin is death" (Rom 6:23).
Question 4. This question touches on the heart of God's dealings with the human race. He has chosen to relate to us by means of a covenant—a contract. We make commitments to him, and he makes commitments to us. Judah and Israel had not kept their end of the deal, and now there are consequences. The good news is that while God is justified in exercising judgment, he also chooses to exercise mercy, keeping his end of the commitment even when we have failed with ours.
Question 5. Clay can't choose to respond to the potter. We can.
Question 6. The quality of answers you get will depend on the trust level of your group. Don't force your group to respond, but allow them time to open up if they are reticent. Be ready to start with your own experience to encourage others to speak up.
Question 8. For more background see Joshua 2:10.
Questions 9-10. God is not eager to judge his people. It comes only because there was a determined resistance.
Question 11. Throughout the Old Testament, one of the primary means of worship and aid to spiritual growth was the rehearsing and celebrating of what God had done for his people. One generation was to tell the next about the great saving deeds of God (Deut 6:10-12; Ps 34; 105; 106).

Study 5. Jeremiah 23:1-24. The Righteous Branch: A Divine Coup.
Purpose: To understand how God rescues his people from bad leadership

by sending Jesus Christ to guide us.

Question 2. The rescue from slavery and Egypt shaped the identity of Israel. Now their return from captivity would become the other signal event in the history of the nation of Israel. God was understood as a God of justice who required obedience, but also as a God who sees the suffering of his people and rescues them from the depth of oppression and pain (Ex 3:7-10).

Question 3. The wisdom of the promised king will have a moral quality about it. He will look at what the situation demands, not merely in terms of what is effective but in terms of what is morally good.

Question 4. The apostle Paul grasped the shocking significance of this phrase. The Reformation was kindled as Martin Luther understood this. God exchanges his moral purity for human immoral corruption (see Rom 10:1-4).

After the return from captivity, Israel became convinced of the importance of the law in a way they had not prior to God's judgment. However, the religious and moral system that grew up around the synagogues looks for righteousness based on a system of human merit rather than a divine gift.

Question 5. When Jesus came as God's Messiah, God's requirement of righteousness came through faith in him. For background read Romans 10:5-13.

There is disagreement among Christian theologians as to how much Jesus' shepherding applies to a literal role in a restored nation. Dispensational theologians look for a physical rulership over a restored Jewish nation that accepts him as messiah. Most reformed theologians feel that this verse is completely fulfilled in the spiritual creation of the church as the new Israel.

Question 6. Jesus declares that he is the good shepherd (Jn 10:1-18). The shepherding role of Jesus is both spiritual and physical. He now shepherds his people by the Spirit until the time that he returns to consummate his kingdom here on the earth (Rev 19—22). At that time his role of leader will be transformed from the land of Judah and Israel to the entire world.

Question 7. The charge of adultery must be understood against the background of the covenant God made with Israel at Mount Sinai. Essentially what took place there was a marriage between God and his people. When Israel began to worship other gods, they were committing adultery and being unfaithful to their marriage vows.

This spiritual adultery led to destructive behavior manifested in poor leadership (v. 1), the misuse of power (v. 10), prophecy by Baal (v. 13) and a refusal to pay attention to the words of God (vv. 18, 22). See 1 Corinthians 1:30.

Question 9. The word *justice* means getting what is deserved. God is showing himself as a just God in shaping a judgment that reflects their failure.

As you read this passage, keep in mind that God is not judging the leaders because they weren't politically good, but because they were morally evil.

Question 10. Encourage people to express themselves, but seek to keep the sharing from becoming a hostile venting of suppressed anger at the leadership of their church.

Question 12. These verses are a challenge for us to spend more time in God's Word while we listen with a quiet and leisurely expectation. The classic understanding of God's communication since the Reformation is that God speaks in his Word by his Spirit. If we want to know what he is saying, then we must study his written Word with a cocked ear to the voice of his Spirit. The Word without the Spirit does not bring the voice of God; we must have words on a page. However, listening to the Spirit without the aid of the written Word leaves us uncertain of what we are hearing.

Study 6. Jeremiah 24. The Basket of Figs: Living with God's Judgment.
Purpose: To understand how God can bless us even in the midst of the most difficult circumstances.

Question 2. Be sure the members of your group get verse 1 clearly in mind. This refers to the first deportation of Judah by Babylon in 596 B.C. The leaders of the nation were the primary targets of the Babylonian army. Everything that takes place in the book of Jeremiah must be understood against this event.

Question 3. It is not that those taken into captivity were any more righteous than those left in Jerusalem. God simply chooses to regard them as good and treat them differently. This is exactly what happens when we believe in Jesus Christ. God changes his regard of us, and we are moved from being considered unrighteous and under his wrath to being considered righteous and extended his grace.

Question 4. This message of support from God is important for two reasons. First, those who were taken would be inclined to feel that they were singled out because they were especially sinful. Second, this pledge indicates that even though the city of God has been invaded, that God himself is still in control. His ability to care for his people is not limited to the land of Judah. There was a belief current in the cultures of that time that when a city had been invaded, the god of that city had been overpowered by the god of the invading people. In addition the power of the gods was considered limited to the geographical boundaries of the country in which they were worshiped.

Question 6. The previous references to "watching" were in regard to judgment. The present "watching" is reference to blessing. Both senses are a fulfillment of God's promise in chapter 1 that he is watching over his Word to see that it is accomplished.

Question 9. The general sense was that the deported ones were under the judgment of God, and those who were left were under his special protection and care.

Question 10. Remember that all the prophecies promised judgment. It now looked like there was a substantial number that had escaped.

Question 11. We can't use outward circumstances to judge how well we are going to do in the light of eternity. Jesus taught that in the coming kingdom "many who are first will be last, and many who are last will be first" (Mt 19:30). This is unsettling if we place our confidence in our abilities, circumstances or anything beyond the grace of God. However, once we give this idea due consideration, it is a source for confidence, humility and gratitude. We are always better off trusting in God's determination for us than anything else in this world or the one to come.

Question 12. Through Christ's work, even death can become a blessing. Martin Luther wrote that when we die in Christ the sting is taken out of death. In this world we have to struggle with sin and spiritual opposition. When we die, we are delivered from decaying bodies and indwelling sin. Death, a curse, in Christ becomes a blessing.

Study 7. The Cup of God's Wrath: International Judgment. Jeremiah 25:15-38.

Purpose: To see how God uses war as a tool for his work in the world.

General Note: This is a hard passage. Don't expect your group to be emotionally encouraged as they work through it. On the contrary, it is difficult, even depressing. The appropriate response is discomfort and pain. The theme of Jeremiah is judgment followed by redemption. We won't experience the impact of Jeremiah's message of redemption until we have faced the terrible depths of sin and God's judgment on it.

Question 3. Nation by nation we get the message that this is an extensive and comprehensive judgment.

Questions 6-7. The sights and sounds of war are a mere reflection of the last battle which will not be between the nations but between God and the human race. Who ever thought that the nations would actually rise up and make war on their Creator? But they will. Since the Fall of the human race way back in the Garden, we have been trying to declare our independence of God. The result has been the widespread, complete and total experience of death. The only variation is in how it comes to us.

Question 8. As with this whole study, this is a hard question. You may get some angry and hostile answers directed at God. That's okay. Don't try to defend God. Encourage and affirm people for expressing themselves. The voicing of concerns opens up the possibility of an interaction with God that will allow him to address those issues in the hearts of the people who raise them.

Question 9. The war in this passage is a judgment on all nations, no matter which side. This was a shocking concept in the ancient world, which thought that the god of the aggressor nation was stronger and extending his power. The Islamic concept of the jihad—holy war—is one incarnation of such thinking that has been present in the Middle East for thousands of years. In contrast, Christians have no concept that justifies the spread of God's power through armed aggression.

Question 11. Throughout history, it has been traditional for nations going to war to claim the blessing of God.

Question 12. God is sovereign even over war. Since he is in ultimate control and has shown himself to be good, just and merciful, we can trust that on the personal or international level all things work together for good to those who love God and are called according to his purpose (see Rom 8:28).

Study 8. Jeremiah 27. The Yoke of Babylon: How to Prosper Anyway.
Purpose: To see how God can bless us in the midst of adversity.

Question 2. A council of envoys from other nations had convened in Jerusalem to discuss how to respond to the Babylonian threat. Jeremiah walked into the summit conference with a yoke on and a message from God.

Questions 4-6. These questions are intended to help the group feel the emotional impact of Jeremiah's message. It went against all common sense. In fact it felt like a call for betrayal of one's country.

Question 7. Jeremiah's words made no sense in the context of those ancient cultures. It was unthinkable that the god of a country would allow himself to be defeated by letting the cities that worshiped him be defeated by a foreign army.

Question 8. Although Judah's citizens were worshiping the Baals, there was also a strong attachment to the temple and the instruments of worship. They didn't reject the Lord and the temple; they wanted him and the Baals too. To have those taken away would be like having the constitution taken away and all the crosses on our churches taken down.

Question 10. Through Jeremiah, God is calling Israel to understand that he is more powerful than they thought. He could send his people into exile and allow the very tools of worship to be taken. But he could bring them back. From beginning to end God is in charge.

Questions 11-12. The confusion of God's sovereignty is that he allows difficult things to happen to his people. The comfort of God's sovereignty is that he is in charge and uses present pain for his glory and our good while promising a future deliverance. God never promises that we will be free from pain, but he does promise that our pain will not be purposeless.

The apostle Paul writes of the comfort that this knowledge brings: "We also rejoice in our sufferings, because we know that suffering produces perseverance; perseverance character; and character, hope. And hope does not disappoint us, because God has poured out his love into our hearts by the Holy Spirit, whom he has given us" (Rom 5:3-5).

Study 9. Jeremiah 28. The Yoke of False Prophets: Destroying False Hope.

Purpose: To expose the dangers of putting our hope in easy solutions or comfort from the wrong sources.

Question 2. Jeremiah was not a popular figure; his message was not welcome. Many saw him as a traitor to the nation.

There were several different prophetic "schools" in Israel and Judah. The canonical prophets represented by Jeremiah, Isaiah and others declared that the righteous character of God required judgment, national defeat and deportation from the land for failing to keep the covenant. The prophets represented by Hananiah maintained that God would not allow his name to be defamed by military defeat. After the invasion by Babylon they changed their tune to say that God would quickly break the power of Babylon and return the exiles. Not surprisingly, the school of prophets represented by Hananiah was much preferred by the nobles and leaders of Judah.

Question 4. Jeremiah takes the opportunity to make it known that he does not enjoy bringing a message of judgment. His response is striking in its lack of defensiveness. He goes on to say that while he desires the good of Judah, his message is in line with what the prophets for the preceding 175 years had been saying: that unless God's people turned away from the worship of false gods, they would be judged.

Question 6. The test of a prophet throughout the nation's history was that what he said had to come true.

Question 7. Hananiah was telling the people that times of peace were impending without any response of repentance. All the prophets of the Lord

(Elijah, Elisha, Amos, Isaiah) called for repentance and exclusive worship.
Question 10. Jeremiah's response is a vivid demonstration of how he stood in the counsel of the Lord. His rebuttal to Hananiah didn't initially include any word from the Lord. Only after he left the scene of the confrontation and heard from the Lord did he deliver a message from God.
Question 11. If the people believed Hananiah, then they were being enticed into false hopes and not open to responding to the call for repentance.
Question 12. God promised to watch over his word and make sure that what was spoken came to pass. What Jeremiah foretold about Hananiah did indeed come to pass—he died.
Question 13. God offers forgiveness and grace to sinners who repent. If we seek to enter into his grace before we have faced our sin, then we keep ourselves from his grace. We are wise to evaluate closely those who offer a painless, effortless gospel.

Study 10. Jeremiah 32:1-25. The Field of Hope: The Promise of Renewed Land.
Purpose: To see that God provides hope in the midst of troubled times.
Question 2. The date is 587 B.C. The Babylonian army has returned and has surrounded Jerusalem, and the city is now in a state of siege. The city of Jerusalem resists for almost two years before it finally falls.
Question 3. This whole experience is a living parable. Jeremiah's ministry is expressed not only in his words but in his life experience. Jeremiah is imprisoned behind walls inside the courtyard of the guard.
Question 5. The purchase of the field continues Jeremiah's ministry as a living parable. He is demonstrating with his own resources that in the face of total defeat by the Babylonians God will return Judah to the land.
Question 6. In the future there would be no question that the field belonged to Jeremiah. During times of siege, such legal details are often ignored as fear increases and public order decays. The whole process would give a sense of comfort and assurance in the midst of the impending defeat, death and destruction.
Question 7. Jeremiah wants God's people to know that he is going to keep his promise that the land belong to the people of Israel in perpetuity. The impending defeat was to be a brief interruption, not a total eradication.
Question 9. Jeremiah would have felt the weight of darkness and death that was soon to overtake him and the city. It's important that we are aware of our own spiritual needs and reach out to God when we need reassurance.
Question 10. Jeremiah rehearses the history of redemption in Israel. God

has a history with Israel of rescuing them from oppression and defeat.
Question 11. Prayer offered against the background of God's gracious work
with his people reminds us of the many times he has come through in dark
times. Prayer not only reminds us of grace but allows us to cast ourselves
upon God for peace and protection.
Question 12. Encourage group members to incorporate passages from
Jeremiah in their prayers. As they do so, they will increase their spiritual
vocabulary for speaking to God and hearing from him.

Study 11. Jeremiah 33. The Sure & Certain Promise.

Purpose: To see that we can trust God to keep his word no matter what our
present circumstances look like.
Question 3. By sending Judah into captivity God's integrity is in question.
He promised the land to Abraham's descendants forever. He also promised
David that one of his descendants would always sit on the throne. God wants
to emphasize that he keeps his covenant despite what the present circumstances look like.
Question 4. The apostle Paul wrote several letters while he was in prison.
In Ephesians 4:1 he refers to himself as a prisoner of the Lord. He knew what
it is like to be confined yet still be free. As with Paul and Jeremiah, we can
trust that God has a purpose for our present situation. While our present
goals and activities may run into a blockage, we can trust that we are on
course to spiritual goals and eternal rewards.
Question 7. God's good reputation brings glory to him and assures us that
it is good to trust him.
   Even though God is concerned about his reputation, keep in mind that
he was not willing to overlook the sins of his people. Despite the impression
that the god of Babylon was stronger than he was, God was willing to use
Babylon as an instrument of his judgment.
Question 9. We have seen the reference to the "LORD Our Righteousness"
(v. 16) once before in Jeremiah 23:6. While Israel failed in their moral
commitment to God, God chose to keep both sides of the covenant commitment, his and Israel's. In Jesus Christ he exchanged our sin for his righteousness. He requires us to be righteous, but forgives us when we fail. What he
does require is not moral perfection, but faith.
Question 11. We take the trustworthiness of God for granted. We shouldn't.
The Judeo-Christian concept of a trustworthy God is not the norm for the
religions of the world. The Greek gods were unsavory and untrustworthy
characters who had to be tricked, overpowered or manipulated by magic if

humans wanted their help.

Question 12. The hope of heaven and the return of Christ are frequently dismissed as pie-in-the-sky by and by. However, the hope of Christ's return and heaven is a strong motivator for those who have the spiritual and moral courage to embrace it. There is a strength in a heavenly hope that allows us to live by our principles without being concerned about immediate responses or setbacks.

Study 12. Jeremiah 38. The Not So Final End: Sunk in the Mud.

Purpose: To consider the need for faithfulness and perseverance in what we believe God has called us to.

Question 2. They don't want any people leaving the city and deserting to the enemy. All hands were needed to stand on the walls and fight.

Question 4. Refer again to Jeremiah's call in chapter 1. God said it was going to be hard and that he would be rejected. God also told Jeremiah that he would need to be strong and not give in to fear.

Question 5. Salvation in a fallen world means a taste of suffering. Paul wrote, "For it has been granted to you on behalf of Christ not only to believe on him, but also to suffer for him" (Phil 1:29).

Question 9. Jeremiah continues to be a living parable. Jeremiah was sunk in the mud but was rescued. If Zedekiah trusted God, even though he was also in the mud of certain defeat, God would rescue him as well.

Question 11. Consider Jeremiah's character and obedience as well as the outcome of his ministry.

Stephen Eyre is a pastor at Crestview Presbyterian Church in Cincinnati, Ohio. He is also the author of Drawing Close to God *and the LifeGuide® Christian Beliefs. He and his wife, Jacalyn, coauthored the LifeGuide* Matthew *and eight Spiritual Encounter Guides.*

What Should We Study Next?

A good place to start your study of Scripture would be with a book study. Many groups begin with a Gospel such as *Mark* (22 studies by Jim Hoover) or *John* (26 studies by Douglas Connelly). These guides are divided into two parts so that if 22 or 26 weeks seems like too much to do at once, the group can feel free to do half and take a break with another topic. Later you might want to come back to it. You might prefer to try a shorter letter. *Philippians* (9 studies by Donald Baker), *Ephesians* (13 studies by Andrew T. and Phyllis J. Le Peau) and *1 & 2 Timothy and Titus* (12 studies by Pete Sommer) are good options. If you want to vary your reading with an Old Testament book, consider *Ecclesiastes* (12 studies by Bill and Teresa Syrios) for a challenging and exciting study.

There are a number of interesting topical LifeGuide studies as well. Here are some options for filling three or four quarters of a year:

Basic Discipleship
Christian Beliefs, 12 studies by Stephen D. Eyre
Christian Character, 12 studies by Andrea Sterk & Peter Scazzero
Christian Disciplines, 12 studies by Andrea Sterk & Peter Scazzero
Evangelism, 12 studies by Rebecca Pippert & Ruth Siemens

Building Community
Christian Community, 12 studies by Rob Suggs
Fruit of the Spirit, 9 studies by Hazel Offner
Spiritual Gifts, 12 studies by Charles & Anne Hummel

Character Studies
New Testament Characters, 12 studies by Carolyn Nystrom
Old Testament Characters, 12 studies by Peter Scazzero
Old Testament Kings, 12 studies by Carolyn Nystrom
Women of the Old Testament, 12 studies by Gladys Hunt

The Trinity
Meeting God, 12 studies by J. I. Packer
Meeting Jesus, 13 studies by Leighton Ford
Meeting the Spirit, 12 studies by Douglas Connelly

Other InterVarsity Press Books and Bible Studies by Stephen Eyre

Drawing Close to God
Quiet Time Dynamics

LifeGuide® Bible Studies
Christian Beliefs
Matthew (with Jacalyn Eyre)

Spiritual Encounter Guides (with Jacalyn Eyre)
Abiding in Christ's Love
Anticipating Christ's Return
Daring to Follow Jesus
Enjoying Christ's Blessings
Entering God's Presence
Sinking Your Roots in Christ
Sitting at the Feet of Jesus
Waiting on the Lord